BUT WHO'S COUNTING?

Zelda Leah Gatuskin

BUT WHO'S COUNTING?

collected poems

Worldwind Books   Albuquerque

Printed in the United States of America
First Printing, 2010
ISBN: 978-0-938513-41-4
Library of Congress Control Number: 2010927020

Publications Acknowledgments:
A Left-Handed Poem, The Year I Will Be Forty I Will
Before, and Crisis were previously published in TIME AND
TEMPERATURE: *thoughts about consciousness*
by Zelda Leah Gatuskin (first edition, Studio Z-Amador
Publishers, 2003). The Tree was previously published in
ANCESTRAL NOTES: A Family Dream Journal by Zelda Leah
Gatuskin (Amador Publishers, 1994).

Worldwind Books
is an imprint of
Amador Publishers, LLC
Albuquerque, New Mexico
www.amadorbooks.com

in memory of my Uncle Irv
Irvin Meyer Citron, 1924-2004

Morphology of the Title

Typically in the context of blintzes or latkes:
"Here, have another"
[plate extended]

"No, no, I've already had ..."
[palm raised to fend off plate]
(four or five or six)

[plate parked in arm's reach]
"...But who's counting?"
[deft stab of fork]

BUT WHO'S COUNTING?

Contents

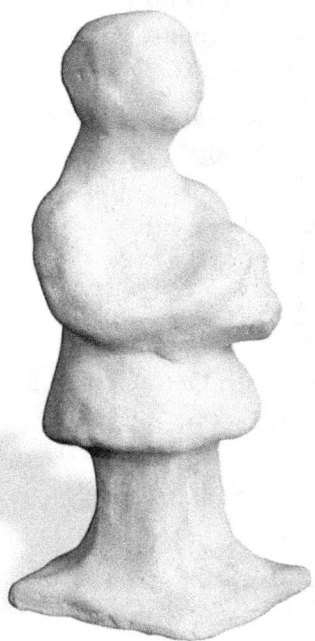

A Left-Handed Poem

plodding
practicing plodding
pretending patience
portending perfection
all it takes is time
all it takes is all we've got
and all we's don't got
all it takes is the cake
all it takes is one false move one mistake
and we're caught
that's what we thought
so long as time retained its image as sequential
take that away and time is just a passing without direction
a sea without a shore
take the ticking of the clock
it never has regrets or fears
if it tires it may stop
or slow or plod or nod
but once wound it repeats *and* moves forward
without regard to which is which
that is practice

The Schwartz Sisters
(for Liz)

For Mom's birthday they will play
Mozart quartets
in her marvelous adobe home
all folksy warmth and airy sunlight
on that flat breezy plain above the Rio Hondo,
after she has fed them.

Tea is served on a milk crate
draped with woven textile, the center
of a four-spoked mandala:
Sister, Sister, Sister, Mom
sitting behind twiggy metal music stands
flourishing long bows with brown arms
voices rising and falling, layered
and so alike, like sisters,
sheet music rustling.

Ani, blackbird, extends her wings
above her four-colored score.
She pulls the bow authoritatively
while her mom plays second fiddle,
nervous, overwhelmed
hands shaking a little.
Suzie, youngest, is on viola
middle daughter Betsy, cello.

From the first chord: Magic!
Mozart dances bow to bow
the tone exquisite between flubs,
squeals, giggles, apologies.
Asides while playing:
"That part's hard!"
"Good job, Mom!"

Betsy becomes entranced, listening
when Amadeus pens a rest.
She nearly forgets her next entrance.
Suzie, serious and strong
is used to keeping up, and then exceeding
as little sisters learn to do.

Ani takes the fancy riffs
perched on one butt cheek
right leg balancing left elbow
the scroll a fifth appendage, the bow a sixth
the violin itself the body of a great musical insect
spinning threads of sound.

And everyone is blissed by
the beats they're leaning into
these four soaring vessels adjusting
their sails by turns, navigating from charts.
What a fortunate wind carries their
harmonies across the prairie sea.

They play and scold and chide and start anew.
Sister, Sister, Sister, Mom
Attaining the final chord of the last movement
someone says, "This is really fun, Mom,
now that you're good!"
and the sisters all burst out laughing.
And Mom could not be more pleased.

Up, Up, Up

My grandmother's a gas
as inhibitions, never very strong
drift away
I always loved her sassy laugh
Now she says
"Sometimes I feel like I'm lifting a million pounds
just to get my big ass out of this chair."

With all due respect
I've seen it bigger
But even while her body curls and dwindles
something which resides within expands
like soap bubbles
Iridescent, untouchable,
light bouncing back in rainbows

"Up, up, up!"
She sings herself to standing
a toddler in polyester slacks
With the mouth of a sailor
"Fuck, fuck, fuck!" she cries in mirth
"I'm so old I can say anything I want and
I think I will before it's too late."

Some bubbles burst
but hers is reaching a point of fullness
from which it may let go
Like a balloon straining at its tethers

We hang on in sheer delight
She dances in our hands
now the woman we knew

Now a silly sprite
When the last molecules unglue
and Grandma's spirit floats aloft
We'll run behind her shadow waving
until she disappears from view

The Year I Will Be Forty I Will Before

This next birthday, I have decided
I will not be forty
I will be four
Will be as I was at four
As I was before

Before ego and self separated
Were socialized
Sanitized
And taught to tell time

I know I couldn't tell time at the age of four
I had no need of it, nor it of me
I noticed light and shadow
In the backyard I sat on a green swath
Watching the white bedclothes sway and ripple
The four-cornered flutterers so blank but so alive
Me too, at four, before

Squirming at the kitchen table,
    I was made to look at the clock
However old I was, it was too old by now
I would learn to read the clock already
Something more than time imposed itself on me
My free-floating mind,
    hitherto anchored by two tipsy clothespins
Now lassoed round and wrestled to submission
You can count, can't you?

You can read the numbers!
One, two, three, four

Before the kitchen clock snatched me up
    in its tireless hands
I was a compact little package,
    curly, pudgy, puckish
All soul and drool
All that was and would be
All of now and never rolled up into
One
...two, three, four...
And do you know your age?
And how many sisters you have?
And what time Daddy comes home?

The year I will be forty I will before
I will snap back the telescope of time
Take out all the space between
    all the layers of all the years
Let them settle softly, one atop the other
If shuffled, all the better
A mess at rest
Remember me?
Tousle-haired, precocious
Time is not true and it's arbitrary besides
I knew this then, better for having all my knowing
Whole if not articulate in my roly-poly being

Expression, others and my own, has stretched me thin
I am bigger but my thoughts are smaller
My sense of self transparent and conditional
Like a see-through plastic ruler
Or the glass-faced clock
But I saw through the friendly assimilation
The time teaching trick to divide my thoughts and conquer
Time is not real, I told myself
So I needn't bide it, or need only
And I haven't and I have
It is now again, the big Now that it was
Before

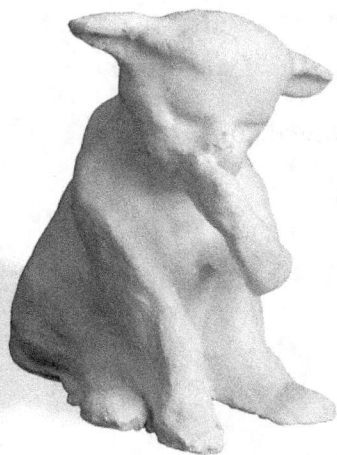

Runes

She is leaving runes now
The long, well-chewed stick
exactly perpendicular to the front door
perfectly centered on the welcome mat
pointing
    this way in
    this way out
with a cow's cervical bone gnawed to a jagged fractal
demarcating the mid-point of her wooden wand
The two objects close
but not touching

    Bone and Stick at Door
Such is the stuff of augury
While I comb the I Ching for clarification I think:
No surprise the pup is prophetic
Didn't I dream dogs until she materialized
on a cold street corner in the dead of winter?

    Fluffball on Sidewalk
You are entering the year of the dog

Local Miracle

Nan was walking the local sidewalks
Instead of the more scenic ditch trail
Because it had rained
And that was not the miracle
Rain is rare here but not unheard of

She saw something pale and round in the gutter
And stooped to see and picked it up
Because it was a baby turtle
And that was not the miracle
Nan is a Buddhist and attends to small things

She held the baby turtle in her palm
Thinking sad thoughts until a tickling
Told her little feet were moving
As baby turtle life expressed itself
And that was not the miracle either

The miracle is that there happens to be a fellow
Nearby who keeps turtles and tortoises
A self appointed rescuer of reptiles
And Nan took her treasure to him
And they named it Dharma

The Scarlet "E"
(for Endangered)

Put yourself in the silvery minnows' shoes
You have a lifespan of, what?
A couple of years?
If you don't get eaten
And you're okay with that
Because you haven't got a clue
What a year is or isn't
What might've been
Or wasn't
Want
Is not exactly in your vocabulary
You are a simply swimming silvery minnow
Without conscious concern for your species
Or your soul

Then you get scooped up
Stoned on some scientist's sleepwater
Injected with a red tattoo
Splashed in saline to soothe the wounds
And resettled upstream
Where your waters and faintly red glowing fellows
Feel different in a way that inflicts
consciousness

All will soon become familiar
As the recurrent fright
Of being caught

Looked at
And returned
Isn't this really more excitement
Than a little fish deserves?

There are some heavy reasons for fiddling with nature
Summed up they have to do with "saving"
But try explaining that to the minnow
Who used to be free to die
And now lives at our pleasure
Under watchful eye

Ethel by Numbers

Ethel's 93
She's lived in the same house
60 years
Her brother's 89
He's lived there with Ethel
Since her husband passed away
That was 16 years ago
Seems they were widowed
About the same time

Ethel's late husband's sisters
Are Sisters
There are 2
Ages 98 and 100
The Sisters
Live at the Mother House
In Cincinnati
When the family learned
The sisters would visit
They all had to come too
That's how Ethel had
17 guests
For Sunday dinner
Which just about did her in

Ethel's not hearing so well
These days
Used to be her eyes

Gave her trouble
12 years
Ago they said
    You better come in and have that checked
    Every year
Last year
They said whatever it was
Was gone
They don't know why
But sure would like to
So they asked Ethel to please keep coming back

Now Ethel has this hearing loss
    Are the ears and eyes connected?
Ethel asks
Implying the ailment simply
Picked up and relocated
Along some cranial path

Ethel drives herself to early Mass
7 days a week
She takes a walk every day
The weather's nice
Ethel tells me
She walked 5 days last week
Today is Monday
And already
She's walked 2 days
Counting today

Ethel plants her stick
Steadies herself by holding onto my forearm
Bringing me close
So she can hear
A private conversation
Under Ethel's broad
Brimmed straw hat
My words suddenly important
Confidential
The weather
The dog

My little ambassador of good will
Millie paws the ground and barks
A greeting
Whenever Ethel nears
    How is your brother? I miss seeing him
I speak of the 89 year old
He also wears a straw hat and
Carries a stick
Though he is tall
While Ethel's tiny

Despite the stick
Millie liked him right off
    My brother?
    He has a treadmill now
    I won't go near the thing
Ethel squeezes my arm

Isn't this weather marvelous?
I've been out walking
2 days this week already
Counting today

The Church of Conrad

He writes his autobiography on the air
Of battles fought, won, lost and drawn
One anecdote at a time
In a thin voice
In a thin pair of jeans
And a sweatshirt so tattered
It looks like it's been peeled off a Siberian mummy

We stand on his Gettysburg
The paved parking lot
Between Episcopal church and
The shaggy shady plot
Where stands his home
On land gentled
But not tamed

And for the longest time
I thought he was nature's guest
An eccentric if not insane
Breaker of twigs
Leaving neat piles of kindling
Up and down the irrigation ditch
To warm his nights under the stars

With the late great dog Storm by his side
He was a semi-threatening figure
Like a scarecrow come to life
That woody bundle

Clutched in each fist...
Is it gathered
From the ground
Or caught
Out of sleeves and cuffs?

Turns out he's landed gentry
With a roof over his head
An old Chevy in the shed
A boat
On blocks
Floating among the weeds
He is not homeless
But one who picks up their trash

He is in no way crazy
But he's mad
Well known at City Hall
The church
Paved over this piece of ditch
A block's worth of walking path tarred
For their parking lot
So his story goes
Standing by their dumpster
And the debris
That overflows from endless expansion

Conrad blew the whistle
Though much damage was already done
Now at least the church
Must tend the Russian Olive trees
They themselves installed
Then deprived of ready water
And the sweetheart deal with that
Construction company across the road
Exposed and nixed
They paved the lot for cheap
Then parked their trucks in it

Conrad shakes his fist
Maintaining a tight grip
On two crushed beer cans
And a burrito wrapper
Without the dog nearby
He looks frail
Installments
In outrage grow
Infrequent

The once ubiquitous figure
Keeps mostly to his own side
Of the Russian Olives now
Though tidy piles of twigs
Still line the ditch
Going north

And the City still hears from him
And the church won't pave more parking lot
So long as he's alive

On Sundays
Latecomers must park along the street
Delivering up
A progressive, generous, do-gooding throng
Who would bulldoze the old man's domain
In a heartbeat
To further the glory of God

God smiles on Conrad
Even as Conrad smiles back a gap-toothed gloat
Clenches trash-laden fingers into fists
And wheezes forth a curse
On the Deity and His monument
Whose shadows fall on
Addicts, prostitutes, runaways
The hungry and homeless
While Conrad cleans up the mess
And preaches by the dumpster
To any who will listen

The Flipping Election

The Dow is up
The Dow is down
The NASDAQ is down
Bonds are up
TVs are on
The votes are in
The votes are out
Bush is up
Gore is down
Gore is up
Bush is down
The count is right
The count is wrong
The numbers don't add up
The markets are falling
The chads are falling
The punch holes don't line up
The Dow is down
Gore is down
Bush is up
The lawsuits are in
The filings are filed
The rulings are ruled
The rulers are worried
Gore is up
Bush is down
The markets are holding
The president is laughing

The lawyers are pleading
The voters are suing
The heads are talking
The judges are juggling
The Dems are dubious
The Repubs are disgusted
Gore is bushed
Bush is gored
The stocks are stalled
The counties are counting
The watchers are watching
The spokespersons are speaking
Mouths are moving
Math is fuzzing
Mud is slinging
Multiple executions take place in Texas
Regrets regrets in Tennessee
Too close to call in New Mexico
A slim margin in Iowa
Mischief alleged in Wisconsin
The Nader factor
The Nader factor
Outrage
Rhetoric
Rush to judgement
Touch football
Band-aid on face
And next up
Experts

Mailbox Moment

The most beautifully lettered envelopes
come from prison
where a man has time
to draw each character
and color it
with a few hard-won markers
miraculously preserved from crazy cellmates
and marauding guards.
The facility provides the stationery
like any good hotel
less the fashionable return address.

As Seen on TV

For fifteen hundred dollars
plus or minus
you can turn your house into a gas chamber.
The Exterminator will come out
with his hard-bodied assistants
who will drape your home
from the roof down
in double-thick, impenetrable plastic tarp.
The hems of the tent will then be sealed at bottom
with long tubular sandbags placed end to end
to end, until back to the beginning
securing the ring of death.
Your termites will then be gassed.
Some time later, the Exterminator will return
and have his muscular minions remove the tent.
Some time after this, you may move back in
and enjoy the comforts of home
letting your mind rest easy now,
now that the dark, crawling host has been eliminated
for good.

Throwing Stone
(West Bank / Sarajevo)

Feel the stone
Smooth and
Hard and
Cool in my right hand
 hand of vengeance
Cool against my feverish skin
 the right size for clenching
Hard against my yielding flesh
 the right size for throwing
Hand holds stone
 hardened heart of rage
Hot veined fingers cradle
Cool unyielding stone
I can feel its weight
Perfectly
Measure with my pulsing veined fingers
Measure in spasms of blood pumping arteries
Its loft
Its arc through the sky
The exact amount of force required
To pull back
 aim
  and release
The exact line of fire
Its loft
Its arc through the sky

The stone throbs
    to be thrown
And my anger
    hard and steady
And my arm
    catapult of steel tendons
The stone's weapon
The stone's tool
The stone throbs
    to be thrown
Tells my hand how to hold it
Tells my arm how to draw back its sinewy bow
Tells my eye how to aim it true

I grip this stone
Inside a storm of stones
Petrified fury
Rain of fists
A river pelted by fear
    splashes back at us
Cry of lament
    chord of mourning
        regret, despair, dismay
How they mock us, our tormenters
If our rage is their food
This stone is manna
Transformed by my hand

into bitter root
dry bread
brine
Pumping nourishment
From fist to heart
Blood mingling with molten rock
Nerves steady as granite

I fear nothing!
With this stone in hand
I am as sure and strong
As I am wronged
I am as certain
as justice
Swift
as revenge
So the stone demands
And my hand listens
So the stone instructs
And my arm imagines
I am the means
to the stone's end

I am held by a stone
Held together
Held in suspension

Suspended by hand
    wrist
        arm
            shoulder
From the mother rock that suckles me
Hard round breast of vengeance
Fills me with power
    Fills me with need
        Fills me with hate
The stone will be thrown
It wills it
It burns the flesh
    once cooled
The stone will be thrown
Will strike its mark
It has taken my eyes for its own
The rage that blinds me
Will power it home

Stone strikes
Target felled
Stone fallen
    finally
        I as well
No longer held
No longer holding
No longer strong

No longer knowing
   why
      or who
Stone leaves hand
All collapse
   weapon
      victim
         victor
Spent and empty
   cold
      alone
Wishing, wishing
Hearts were stone

Rags to Rags

My great-grandfather walked away
from the profitable family printing business in Poland
to seek his fortune in the USA
He, and an adventurous cousin who found his niche
in pocketbooks

Dov Berish handled this and that
worked his way down
from New York to Atlanta
from printer to peddler
became Bernard

His American-born children especially
grew up ashamed of their father's failure to profit
in this rich land
He remained a poor rag merchant
to his humble, early end

But Bernard provided
if poorly
for four offspring and a wife
while the rich Polish people
perished

Where did the wealth go?
To hell, for all Bernard cared,
    "To Hell with it!"
He took the money for printing press parts

and bought a passage
later brought his family

So I get to be here with my rag collection

I wonder why I keep these old jeans and tattered tunics
What use the frayed bedsheets, holey socks,
    torn undershirts?
Some use, I think
much, perhaps
in these high grade cotton rags

When the economy collapses and the power flickers out
on that day when we get to start over re-inventing civilization
these old rags might be my gold
Such hand-me-down crafts as stitchery and thrift
    and wit
might sustain me

All this and a deep curiosity
about the life of a man
who made too small a success
to become a bragged-about patriarch
He left others to fulfill his dreams

An early photo shows the ungrateful heir
posed in a Serock, Poland studio
wearing a good cap and overcoat

with neat beard, no sidelocks
and an inscrutable expression

Do I read defiance in those eyes?
Anxiety?
He may simply be trying hard not to crack up laughing
an expression I have seen on my uncle's face
when he's supposed to be being serious

It would be all right to laugh now, Bernard
So far, things have turned out okay
And for the uncertain future... I have my rags
It's a real useful thing, a rag
I'm saving mine for the end of the world

The Tree

He is not an old man
Just a tired man who feels old
As he trudges home from a ten-hour workday
Six days a week he works
Taking only the Sabbath off
And he remembers when he had to work seven
It didn't matter then
About the Sabbath
And the old ways
To his wife, to his mother
But not to him
For whom the magic of the ritual
Had been left behind on the other side of an ocean
Along with his childhood
He is not an old man
Just one who got off to an early start
In the responsibility department

Six days a week, ten hours a day, he works
Yet still he sits long into the night
Reading and studying
As he was taught to do in his grandfather's house
Where a printing press shared residence
With the family's pet goat
He hungers for knowledge
The long days of tallying accounts
Leave him empty, numbed

As he rounds the corner to his street
Does his step quicken in anticipation
Of the hot meal on the table
Or of the paper-wrapped books expected
    from the postman?
Like grandmother's goat he will devour anything
Pulp novels, physics textbooks...
He belongs to the synagogue, the book club
He has his family, and, when he's lucky, a job
Yet within himself he feels alone
He needs rest, but craves the energy to do more
Work puts food on the plate
Sleep makes work possible
But work and sleep do not make a life
A good wife makes the home a palace, a sanctuary
Healthy children honor the past
Carry the family names into the future
But a man should not have to choose between
Supporting his family and enjoying their company

Here, here is his yard
The house he toils to keep
But all is not right this evening
Look, that limb still hangs dangerously from the linden tree
The men did not come as scheduled to remove it
He scowls
What's the use of laboring to keep a roof over their heads
If a heavy branch is waiting to fall on them
In their own front yard?

He straightens, invigorated
See, he is needed here
Earning a paycheck is not all that a husband does

He slips into the house
She is out
Of course, it is *Tisha b'Av*
A day of mourning and sadness
She fasted today and is at the Temple now
He sighs
I work all day for the *goyim*
And she prays all day to God
Meanwhile, Mother Nature will send this tree
Down upon our heads
Well, not if I can help it
Saw in hand, he returns to his yard and climbs the tree
And why not?
He is not an old man
In fact, he feels younger by the minute
Sawing away at the cracked limb that now looms
    in his mind
As an assassin
The threatening branch crashes to the ground
He remains in the tree
The long summer dusk soothing him
The cool broad linden leaves brushing his cheeks
So hot from exertion
Stars appear

He sees them as the twinkling eyes of angels
And feels blessed here in his lovely tree
His fine house awaiting his repose
His wife on her way home to him
Tonight, instead of picking up his book
He will ask her to sing to him the songs of their youth

But, descending the tree is much harder than climbing it
The day's long hours wash over him
His heart beats wildly
Between fighting the weary feeling
And rejoicing in the vanquishing of the branch
He enters the house clutching his chest
And staggers to his bed
He wants to take off his shoes but cannot
The room spins, becomes the starry sky,
A blur of linden leaves
Come, Come, the angels sing
No, no, I am not an old man, he gasps
Wait, wait

Her face
She is there
Her face one last time
Her face
Tears
I'm so sorry, my *feygeleh*, so sorry
But at least I leave you on *Tisha b'Av*

And you will not have to mourn an extra day of the year
for me
Es iz bashert...
Her face
Tears
Stars
Linden leaves
The voices of angels
Come, come

Pow Wow Weekend

I.

It's late Thursday afternoon
Weeks after we were sure
Well, hoped
The spring winds had passed
A breeze lifts
Gathers
A large man in a long cape
Making ready
Elm seeds rise into gold-dusted air
Windows rattle
Newly leafed limbs slap at each other like fussy children

Comes this cloud of fine sand
Gathered earth of bosque, mesa
Indian Country beyond
Arizona
The Mojave
The mini twister
Dust Devil, we call it
Dervishes up the street pulling the winds with it
Until its tail of breeze flicks out of sight

Air clears and stills
Rodeo tonight

II.

Next day
Friday
Same time of day
That distant moan swelling to howl
The elm seeds eddying up Central
Forecast another gale
But gusting through without much force
Only a breathless straggler racing to the arena

Fringes of showers skitter high out of reach
Evening throbs with the resonance of drums
Nations and elements are gathered

III.

My car won't start in the morning
Its battery drained of power
Like so many listless limbs
All energy has been drawn to the circle
Gathered up
Summoned to the vortex

With great effort we are able to move by noon
We two heaps
And the city seems strangely quiet
For a Saturday

With 50,000 visitors gyrating
At the epicenter of a prayer

Only at nightfall does the sky, seeded by dance
Open
Pulses quicken with that good steady not-too-hard rain
Warm night walking
Water halos in our hair
Moist breathing
Renewal

IV.

Sunday sparkles
Rain washed, sun dried
Weary in that good kind of way
Air so clear
The train whistle resounds like a pipe organ
Beneath a blue dome of cloud-puffed sky
Cloud-like
Small gatherings scatter and regroup
For family time, feasting, farewells
Day dozes off into full-bellied dreams

Evening awakens to howling winds
The gathered forces disburse
Race home on a current that blows loud and hard
All night

V.

And all next day
The swirling tumult
Badgers workaday Monday world
With spirit breath
And the beating of Eagle wings

The Fool

What I feared
Eventually
Inevitably
Happened, in a dream
A dog chased me
I stopped, turned toward it
And commended myself for being unafraid
The dark form lunged, teeth bared
I held my ground, stood calmly
It reached me, furious but confused
Not so vicious, I thought
And commended myself for being unafraid
Then the beast put its teeth
Very delicately
Very deliberately
On my bare ankle, as if to say,
Run, you fool, run!

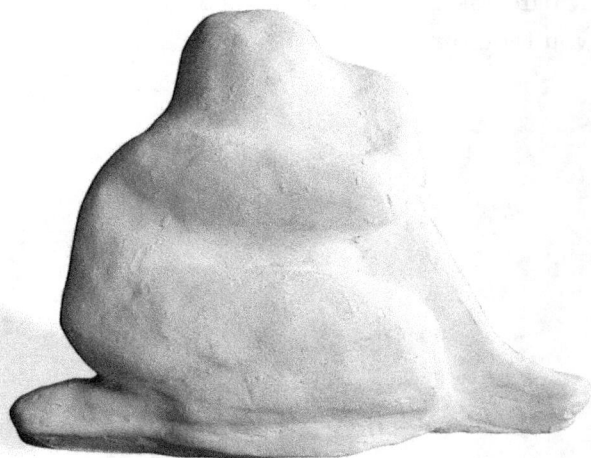

Crisis

a crisis is a crisis is a crisis
but a crisis is not hopeless
one comes through it
if it wasn't an ordeal, a complete shake-up
it wouldn't be a crisis
one comes through it
did I say I wanted off the grid
this will do it
sleep and meals, work and play interrupted
by phone calls that cannot wait
be ready to fly at any moment
I am ready now, would willingly
but am stuck in pending mode
it would not serve the cause to panic
what good would it do for me to disobey
or at least assert
for me to display how much I hurt

three days and two thousand miles later —
six things to do when your dad has a coronary:
1. notice that things that seemed important are nct
2. pack
3. redefine the word Future
4. grow up already
5. get ready to believe in God
6. pray

what to pack for the hospital waiting room:
quarters for the pay phone
tissues
tums
books you won't read
snacks you won't eat
a sweater
and vitamin C
for courage

Today's Nuclear Family

Going from parking lot
To hospital
A pungent waft of black manure
Mounded in the medians
It's mulching month
Kids hold their noses
Coming out a little girl screams
"I want my mommy!"

Mother, may I?
My daddy gets to leave
The massive fortress
For a smaller
Nearer rehab center
One giant step closer
A lighter hand on the landscaping
Sunshine tulips against velvety pansies

Funky smells saved for
Hallways full of doors
Embarrassingly open
Here independence is the goal
Not sterility
Struggle is allowed
You want out?
Walk, baby, walk

PT sounds good to me
Our neighbor used to be a tall man
Today I greet him
At eye level
He's so bent
But still mowing his own lawn
It's the first push of this
Yellow-purple spring

In the house once removed
With all the cars out front
A new baby
Proudly on display
Swinging widely
In the picture window
All alone
A second ago

Someone gave his baby bucket
A big push
And went away
Across the street a crow
Marches up the walk
Like he owns the place
Rattling his keys
Under his wing

Forsythia and flowering plum
Spring

Our little development is shaped
Like a sputum bowl
A redundancy of sloping
Arcing lanes
Which cannot be walked all the way
Without retracing steps

On the outside curve
A family confers at the curb
Dad's bald
And son's shaved heads
Hover like Easter eggs
Above the mower
Dandelion and violet tufts
Soon to be shorn like the men

Everyone envies green
Believes in keeping colors
In their place
The man with the big corner lot
Wears a mask while he toils
Do not breathe the grass
Mowing mowing
Mulching mowing

Rounding the inside curve
Kids on bikes
Kids with walkie talkies
Woman with too small wheelbarrow

And two big heaps of soil
Smack in the driveway
Trapping cars in the garage
Making Monday loom large

Everyone's in t-shirts
I wear a
Just-in-case-it-rains
Plastic jacket
From the hall closet
Me and my precautions
Getting moist
On the inside

Buttery daffodils and
What are those called?
With the clusters of vivid bells?
Phlox? Hyacinth? Ah well
In the purple-yellow drama
Of the moment
Let me not omit the pinks
From this suburban scene

Weeping cherry
Crabapple
Dogwood
Other pastel-petaled puffs
I never learned the names of
And slices of crimson

Azaleas and rhododendrons
Just budding

Spring
By the time I lap myself
The baby's been put away
The swing
Hangs heavier without him
My tour of thirty-five years complete
I take borrowed keys from borrowed pocket
And let myself back in

Upstairs in Grandma Sadie's old room
In Sadie's chair
My feet on Sadie's footrest
Reflecting
Sparrows flap around the window
Nesting between sill
And air conditioner
While the trees still lack leaves

Making the best of things
Spring
It's almost time to go back
To Dad
To watch him struggle with supper
While we sit on our hands
Counting down the days
To homecoming

Short Ride with Detour

On the platform
Four out of fourteen people
Talk on cellphones
One reads poetry
That's me
Fighting to hold my mental ground
Against a soft insistent voice nearby
Woman in black coos
Her tone professionally modulated
 How are you set there?
 Do you have some time?
 A little tricky the way
 Sue set up the billing
 Would you?
 Here's what we need...
She wears shiny black open-toed shoes
Showing shiny red toenails
She has diamonds on her watchband
Gold monogram on her sunglasses
Success is her middle name
Is there a minute of the day
When she is not thinking work?
Only her bare toes notice
The warm spring breeze

On the train
The seats are two across
In my row

One out of every two people
Talks on a cellphone
One writes a poem
That's me
Scribbling to stay front of
A conversational fault line
But slipping
The tiny-voiced traveler insists
    I *can hear* you *fine*

Stupid things always steal my attention
She looks like a kid
Black stretchy-lacy top and blue jeans
Blue backpack at her feet
Playing pretend business
    Yeah, it was okay
    We got our fill of curry
    He didn't seem to want to do anything
    More into the companionship
I'm hooked again
Man invites girl for business lunch
At which he will not do business
Girl makes call on cellphone
To comrade who cannot hear
    No no, don't, I *can still hear* you...
Thoughts skitter into the widening abyss
Dragging the poem with them
When the connection terminates
She calls me Ma'am and

Climbs across to go
To the café car
Leaving me
One out of one
Primitive woman with pen
An untraceable call
A runaway train

So very sorry...
She returns with a burger
To put a bottom on the curry
And refrains from dialing until
I stand
Quick draw
The device is at her ear
Before I have swung my suitcase from the rack

'Scapes, 3500 ft.
(for Frank)

Escape! Flight! Piercing the plane of everyday
    where none ascend but we
    to view the igloo-yness of a
    cumulating white
    in bright fulminations
    of snowy mesas
    and confectionery seas

My old blue sleeping bag has burst its cotton stuffing
    releasing childlike leapings across
    mind-sculpted scenes
    a factory of fantasies
    unpeopled but for fellow
    smidgy-widgy things
    with wings
    and memories

Its azure casing floats smoothly above the fluff
    an endless canvas of
    dreams reprised
    wishes granted
    all the magic I once knew come true
    like Cinderella placing both her shoes
    on a conveyor belt
    picking them up on the other side
    and wearing them home to you

39 Suspect Word(s) Found

my spellchecker doesn't recognize
burrito or
burger or
baggie
let alone *ziplock*
or *zonked*

it's not just a prude
it's unpoetic
rejecting
abloom bitty cul-de-sac
and
ditsy
emboldened
footsies
glugged and *grungy*

Holler hollers hollered hollering
do you hear me?
all nixed
nixed it likes
wouldn'tchya know
yeah, *wouldn'tchya*

"Jeez, what a klutz!"
that'll get you:
"2 suspect word(s) found"
nyeh nyeh nyeh

oops
it hates repetition

the fact is
this software is passé
there is no
laptop nerd psycho subtext vibes or
velcro
can you imagine the bleakness of this world?

alas
my *spellchecker* suffers
a still crueler fate
it even suspects itself

bummer

Rabbi Rich's Baggie Full of Wisdom

Before we could go into
Johnny's Dog House
Rich had something to give me
A little dyed-green feather
from a folk instrument
A drum or rattle,
the name escapes me though he said it several times
And that of the person who played it
who was special to Rich
And now I've got the feather

The feather came out of a one-quart ziplock bag
Along with an envelope containing photos
Two each for me, my two sisters, and Mom and Dad
That's four sets of two pictures each with two people:
My mom and Rich's mom and my dad and his dad
He counts and recounts the photos
There's an extra set for his sister
The happy elderly faces in pairs in his lap
repeating like a hall of mirrors

It takes a lot of shuffling through the contents
of the stuffed ziplock
to find the feather and the photos of our folks
When Rich is finished the baggie goes with us
into Johnny's
And sits quietly next to Rich's elbow
while we eat hot dogs and onion rings

With lemonade for me and an "Arnold Palmer" for him
That's half iced tea and half lemonade
Everything's got a name at Johnny's
Maybe they'll name the veggie dog "and clean the griddle"
for me

Once our trash is all cleared away the baggie perks up
under Rich's scrutiny
Poking through a big wad of papers, sifting for gold
He leaves a few scraps on the table
and reloads the baggie
A photo facing out on each side
Through the pockmarked plastic: his young self
on stage behind a big drum kit
He played with some big acts back in the day
"Cool," I say, passing back the bundle
forgetting names like I always do

Now come the writings
Rich reciting the pedigree of each one
he pushes toward me
Quotable quotes, song lyrics
Prayers translated from the Hebrew
Along with Rich's own riffs on inspirational verse
The meaning of the words
becomes obscured by my impressions:
How the downward slant of Rich's mangled printing
fights against those uplifting phrases
The wobbly letters, the tattered pages

the scratched and smudged baggie
All seem to have been to battle
to be doing battle daily against that descending scrawl
But it's easy to see which side is winning
by Richie's smile
I slide the slips of wisdom back across the table
and tell him my woes

Poetry Night

The first poet
had filled his pockets
with smallish pebbles
which he winged at us hard
Pop Pop Pop Pop
and faster
PopPopPopPopPopPop
and every one hit its mark
We were bruised some
but appreciative

The second poet carried a
notebook full of loose leaves
They fluttered up
when she shuffled them
then drifted gently
down about our heads
We couldn't catch them all
but felt the ticklish wind
when they floated near

The next poet
much to our surprise
released birds
so we might observe their flight
accompanied by song
and the occasional
mating call

The poet after this
wore bells on ankles and wrists
each one with a special tone
denoting a color
and dispensing the fragrance
of a cherished place
This we have no idea how she did
She left us with a waft of piñon
and mountain juniper

My turn came
I had nothing up my sleeve
but dreams
a pocketful of question marks
and a stone in my shoe
But all the pretty birds
and leaves and things
came to rest upon my curly head
reminding me that
poetry is inheritance
not sport

Poet In a Box

There is something so inspiring
about this silent antiseptic room
that I must climb down from the
paper draped examining table
clutching my paper wraps around me
so my bare ass
won't be pointing at the door
when it opens
which it doesn't
to fish a writing implement out of my purse
under my pants
and clamber back up on the table
clutching a pen and this magazine
close the paper blouse over my breasts
drape the paper sheet over my lap
and write a poem in the margins
about waiting
about margins
about poems
about the secret place I have brought
to be examined
and the multiple forms completed
by hand by dedicated women
and layered atop other forms
with all the same answers to
all the same questions
as have been asked before

as if the words have anything to do
with what will be found
or combined add up to an incantation
for cellular consistency
That's what I'm wishing for

And on the form it says
I don't have to be here yet
and the priestess of blood pressure bands
and thermometers asked
why I came early
and I said
I didn't expect to get an appointment
so soon
the dentist booked two months ahead
So I'm waiting prematurely
it would seem
But perhaps it is intended
that I pass two months right here
like a deli sandwich in white paper
until my annual truly comes around
in which case
that's a lot of poetry
and not enough margins
But the door is still not opening
so I cast around for more material
and wonder if I should put my
clothes on and go take a pee

after which I might simply
proceed to the exit
because I think the secret
has been discovered
and I don't need to spread my legs
to know what a treasure
this quiet privacy to write

(Here the nurse practitioner enters
just when I was getting warmed up
and now it is later
returning to the scene mentally
wondering if I were to swathe my naked body
in giant napkins
might the poem continue
It was going somewhere
in fact it was going here
to now
when I would be
free
clothed
dignified
mobile
and so I am
but That moment is past
and there is no continuing
Then I was waiting but I was doing
Now I am doing

but I am waiting
for a feeling
to impel me
to write
But wait...

Ka-THUNK!
right outside
strange sound too close
And I step to the window to see a squirrel dive
onto the driveway and run toward the house...
Excuse me...

Yes a squirrel
it raced onto the front porch
trapped momentarily between the wrought iron
and a screen that keeps the dog from escaping
I thought the dog might be involved
but she'd been sleeping
when the squirrel
wisely skirted the yard to cross
above on the studio roof and leap
to the metal casing of out-jutting swamp cooler
hence the noise
and a toasty surprise for the squirrel I bet
And so around it went
through that treacherous porch to the tall junipers
and continued up to our roof and across to the neighbor's

and over and down into old Mrs. Montoya's
old piñon pines
a squirrel oasis
now that I think about it
you don't see many squirrels in the desert

So maybe that mammal went where it oughtn't
but by wit and courage he made it home
and this poem will too
even if we have to burn our toes along the way
and jump about a bit
because if I really had been swathed in paper
I'd not have stepped outside to watch the show
no I don't think so

But
being artistically naked
presenting myself to the world
in my mind's eye
like a fresh baked good
on its sanitary leaf of waxed tissue
unembarrassed
unashamed to show my squirrel
—that's what I'm here to do after all—
has forced the poem
yes forced
like blooms in a hothouse
me on the examining table

boxed in
bored
verging on bitter
white paper everywhere
and coaxed
compelled
to create)

Punctuation of the Womb

Any period could be my last.
The final final period.
For now though, they are but ellipsis points.........
At increasingly irregular intervals. .   .   .
A thought petering out. .   .   .   .
Eventually I suppose I'll start a new paragraph...
No rush, my dears,
We all know where that one ends.

Progress

Studying a younger me preserved in film
I see I've had my youth and then some
extending a school-girl appearance
by refusing to wear lipstick
or stylish shoes

Or to have my hair styled
that dark mass left long and secured with
barrettes or an always-askew bandana
I notice I had bad skin and a
too-thin, pointy chin

Somewhere in my late thirties
I was perfect
before the jowls set in, before glasses
sporting a few distinctive streaks of grey
to lend an air of maturity

So I didn't look like I would simply blow away
on the breeze
a skinny bit of brunette fluff suffering
under the misconception of being both
overweight and a heavy thinker

I'll have to think about that each time
I confront in the mirror my
squarish jaw and silver mane
Click, shudder

What will the future me see:

"You call that jowly?"
"You were just a babe!"
Or at any rate I'll simply
eradicate the double chin
digitally

The Age of Discouragement

Middle age, I decided
at the tender age of forty-two
is the point at which you have begun more projects
than can possibly be done
in double the years
which doesn't preclude starting new ones
or finishing some
but does demand an existential view:
Quit counting and do each thing for
its worthiness in the Now.

Now some years have passed
not so many as to place me squarely
in the "second half"
but enough to make me laugh at myself
and how I felt the stages of aging
related to worries and work
when clearly the real deal has to do with
weight, as in gaining
hair, as in greying
and motivation
as in waning.

Sadie always said
Life Begins at Fifty
for a woman
at least it did for her
which means I must be nearing the end of this

not-quite-life.
Indeed I feel the deadness
of certain false desires
the diminishing of wishes
and a creeping cynicism
one shade darker than is popular.

I have reached
The Age of Discouragement
to become
a burgeoning curmudgeon
bemoaning all the follies of
our cruel species.
For instance:
The brains of fundamentalists
are their own best evidence
for the lie of evolution,
but how to explain the thumbs?

Deeply, deeply discouraged
but not unhappy in the way of wanting things
that typified my youth.
Or impatient. Things can wait.
Besides, even in my underachieving
I am terribly efficient.
Another ten minutes then...
I snuggle my chubby tummy
against my hubby's buns
at liberty to be content.

Whole Lot of Everything
(for Harry)

There's an airplane
Every time I look up
Whole lot more than used to be
But yesterday it was birds
I noted
Whole flocks moving down for the winter
Robins and starlings, crows and grackles
Whole lot of grackles
Whole lot of bird sounds in general

If you listen
Listen for the sandhill cranes
Canada geese high above
Whole lot of migration
While pets stay put
Dogs barking and running up and down
Beside their fences
Lucky ones like Millie getting walked
Cats crossing quiet streets
Checking out each others' yards
Whole lot of cats
For out in plain sight

Whole lot of trash
That never goes away
Unless it blows away
But still it's trash, somewhere else
The persistence of trash

Dusty, brittle, breaking, bleaching
Still there in the weeds
Under the trees
Pile of clothes from a homeless encampment
Now part of the landscape
Swirly blue glass baubles of a broken bong
Splintered planks from a treehouse
A plastic hamper lid
Some of it's been there for years
Whole lot of years

Whole lot of seasons
Whole lot of things changing
That place used to be all run down
Now it's a palace
That was a vacant lot
Now it's a big ugly house
Whole lot of adobe
That was the house where the turtle guy lived
That was Nan's house
After many seasons of study
She shaved her head and donned maroon robes
To become the Buddhist nun Malaya
We would stop to talk or walk a ways together
Until the season in which Malaya died
Others came and went
Others died or threatened to
Whole lot of tears

Whole lot of laughs
Whole lot of doggy antics
Whole lot of sniffing
Cut grass, roasting chile, wood smoke
Someone's doing laundry
Someone's making bacon and eggs
"Noses up," I tell Millie, lifting mine
Whole lot of blue sky
Whole lot of beauty
Whole lot of feelings
Whole lot of thoughts
Whole lot of wonder
Whole lot of love
Whole lot of everything

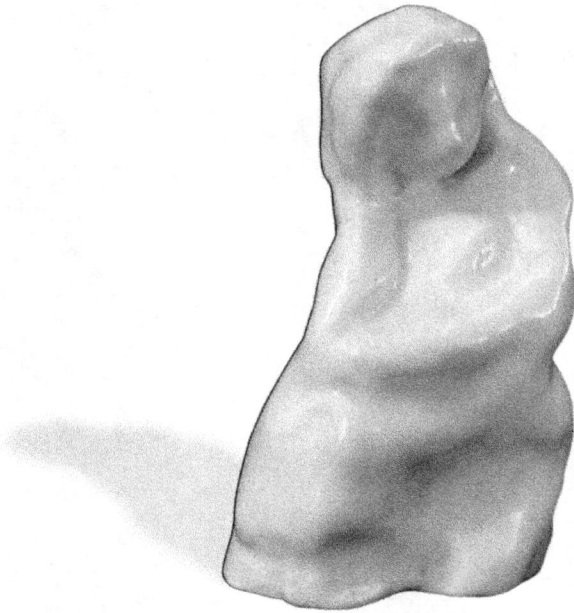

About the Author

Zelda Leah Gatuskin resides in Albuquerque, New Mexico. She is the proprietor of Studio Z, multi-media arts and editor in chief of Amador Publishers, LLC. Her published works include two fantasy novels, THE TIME DANCER and CASTLE LARK, and two collections of creative non-fiction which she also illustrated, ANCESTRAL NOTES and TIME AND TEMPERATURE.

About the Artist

Sadie Temkin Gordon (1904-2000) was born in Boston, MA to recently-arrived Russian immigrants. Though her formal education was limited, she received art lessons at an early age. She pursued her love of the arts throughout her long life, creating hundreds of functional and decorative objects, sometimes with the help of her husband Julius, who was himself a talented woodworker. She considered herself always a craftswoman and a student of art, not a professional or fine artist. A more detailed biography and a digital portfolio are available at http://www.ancestralnotes.com.

All of the art for this book was derived from the works of Sadie Gordon and photographed by her granddaughter, Zelda Gatuskin. Cover: "Fall in Wilmington" oil on canvas board, 1971. Interior art: small clay sculptures and plaques, undated.

www.ingramcontent.com/pod-product-compliance
Lightning Source LLC
LaVergne TN
LVHW021541080426
835509LV00019B/2772